MW01247886

Savage
ANGEL

*A guide to battle spiritual warfare in the
courtroom by putting on the full armor of God*

DANA HANUSZCZAK

Trilogy Christian Publishers

A Wholly Owned Subsidiary of Trinity Broadcasting Network

2442 Michelle Drive

Tustin, CA 92780

Copyright © 2024 by Dana Hanuszczak

All Scripture quotations, unless otherwise noted, taken from *The Holy Bible, King James Version*. Cambridge Edition: 1769. Used by permission. All rights reserved worldwide.

All rights reserved, including the right to reproduce this book or portions thereof in any form whatsoever.

For information, address Trilogy Christian Publishing

Rights Department, 2442 Michelle Drive, Tustin, CA 92780.

Trilogy Christian Publishing/ TBN and colophon are trademarks of Trinity Broadcasting Network.

For information about special discounts for bulk purchases, please contact Trilogy Christian Publishing.

Trilogy Disclaimer: The views and content expressed in this book are those of the author and may not necessarily reflect the views and doctrine of Trilogy Christian Publishing or the Trinity Broadcasting Network.

10 9 8 7 6 5 4 3 2 1

Library of Congress Cataloging-in-Publication Data is available.

ISBN 979-8-89333-939-0

ISBN 979-8-89333-940-6 (ebook)

To my children:

Mommy will never give up!

Because it happened to me too…

These are the things I learned on my path. Things I wish I knew then.

You are NOT alone. You are NOT crazy…

Spiritual Warfare is REAL.

~

I wrote this book with the help of the Holy Ghost and I reference The King James Version of the Bible. I pray that every soul that reads this book shall come to know God and be saved. I pray for you to have an experience with the fire of God; I pray that by the time you finish reading it, you will KNOW that YOU KNOW YOU SERVE A MIGHTY GOD and you trust that in this season of your life, no matter what it is, that God's will prevails EVERY TIME! No matter what it is, it is His will that wins over the plans of the enemy. This book can be applied to any battle in your life. Hallelujah, in the mighty name of Jesus we pray, amen.

TABLE OF CONTENTS:

CHAPTER 1:

Full Armor of God

EPHESIANS 6:11-12:

"Put on the whole Armor of God, that ye may be able to stand against the wiles of the devil. For we wrestle not against flesh and blood. But against principalities, against powers, and the rulers of the darkness of this world, against spiritual wickedness in high places."

God is telling us right here to put on the full armor given to you by Him. Not on your own. He is saying we should trust Him and feel safe knowing He is with us. And knowing that He is God, HE will keep us safe! But He is also letting us know that the devil is coming. He seeks to kill and destroy God's people. But most importantly, he runs the world we live in. Which also includes the courthouses, the judges, lawyers, the children's advocates, etc. So we must, at all times, be fully covered by the blood. We must be with God and keep Him at the center of everything. So what is "The full armor of God?"

EPHESIANS 6:13-18:

"Wherefore take unto you the whole armor of God, that ye

*may be able to withstand in the evil day, and having done
all, to stand. Stand there, having your loins girt about with
truth, and having the breastplate of righteousness; And your
feet shod with the preparation of the gospel of peace. Above
all, taking the shield of faith, wherewith ye shall be able to
quench all the fiery darts of the wicked. And take the helmet
of salvation, and the sword of the spirit, which is the word
of God. Praying always with all prayer and supplication
in the spirit, and watching thereunto with all perseverance
and supplication for all saints."*

As hard as it may seem, we have to be calm, cool, and collected during these battles. I found the only way I had peace and could remain calm while on trial with Satan himself was to constantly be in prayer. I also fasted. I honestly did not have a strong foundation rooted in the church. I didn't attend church before this time in my life, other than briefly during my childhood. This is where I REALLY found God: going through family court and dealing with the thought of losing my child to their abusive dad. It was through these trials that God taught me faith. I remember long nights when I cried so much, thinking, *How could this be happening to me, again?* I was a good mom. I had a great job. My kids loved me. Then I also realized how many other people were in this very same battle. The courthouse is always full of distraught families, begging to be heard. Scared of losing their children. Or scared to let the child go on visits with their abusers. In some cases children are being sexually assaulted by their parent. So I begged to understand why so many of us were here. Why would God allow these things to happen? And where was He through all of this?

But after reading the Bible every day and going to church. I started learning the truth about God. My mind started to shift. I began to get stronger in my confidence. I started to understand there is power in that Book. I cried out to God to show me signs that would tell me that I was truly "saved," really "His," and most of all worthy of His love. I wanted to know God. I needed to know that He was real and with me on this journey. In my situation, since my abuser could no longer harm me, he began to harm our child. He even threatened to kill our child. He said he would throw him off the George Washington Bridge! He actually had a plan! I canceled that plan of the enemy and I prayed and fasted that he would NEVER have unsupervised visits with our child again. I just could not understand how my child's father could threaten to kill his own son. I knew he really meant it too. I remember the very next court date, the lawyer on the opposing side said that I was a bad mom and that because my child was in Cub Scouts and was at a shooting range, I was training him to kill his Father! Then she said I was a "Crazy Christian" and I was in a cult! This lawyer began to attack everything about me.

I began to pray in my head, and I was binding Satan and every plan and sending it back to "Drylands." At that very moment, we were sitting in a side room having a conference but God took me into the very courtroom in my mind. He showed me that it said "IN GOD WE TRUST" on the wall and immediately I felt calm and peace ran through my veins. Like I could actually feel my blood pumping freshness throughout my body. I could feel the warmth of God's love. It was the confirmation I had been waiting for. God began to speak to my spirit! It changed my whole demeanor. I started to understand what it was to have "The Full Armor of God" on. I would not allow those demons to trigger me anymore. It was like I could feel the helmet appear on my head to protect my mind, mostly my own thoughts. The breastplate of righteousness covered my heart, keeping it safe and stopping it from pounding out of my chest. The belt of truth, which was buckled around my waist. And those boots of my salvation were being laced up! It was the peace of God. It felt like I could actually feel the laces being tied on the boots. I had faith that God was not only with me, but I truly believed it was His will that would prevail. Miraculously, I was charged with an electricity that only God could provide. I felt the power of God. I started to believe the words of God spoken over my life. Then finally my lawyer spoke up and fought for me. He began to attack and tear down every lie that was being said about me.

Then we were ordered to go into the waiting area. As I sat down with the ACS worker, (administration for children's services) I could hear a woman singing. She sounded like an angel. "What a beautiful name, the name of Jesus." She was singing so loud, it was disturbing the ACS worker. Laughing inside, I sang along with her. She sounded so beautiful. I could not see her or what she looked like, but I was praising God along with her. Finally, curiosity got the best of me and I got up to look around to see just who had this angelic voice, and to my surprise, there was no one there. I felt puzzled. I know I heard someone singing. I know the ACS worker heard it too because she began to complain about the singing. But when I looked around, the only people in the courtroom waiting area were me, the ACS worker, and my abuser. Huh, so who was singing?

Could it have been an angel for real? I know that ACS worker heard it too. Because she was annoyed with her singing and began to muffle stuff under her breath. Like "Oh, shut up already." Well to God be all the glory. I believed it had to be an angel of God who came along with God that day in the courtroom. But most importantly, I began to understand God was hearing my cries. I began to change inside and out, starting to trust that God was actually with me. I believed my prayers were working. I had power in my prayers. God cared enough about me to listen and to answer. But most of all, God was showing up to my battles.

CHAPTER 2:

Weapons of War!

PROVERBS 31: 26:

*"She opened her mouth with wisdom;
and in her tongue is the law of kindness."*

I began to understand my position and how to play it. Wanting to be constantly present with the Holy Ghost, I began to search the Bible for verses I could lean on when times were tough. Little did I know, I was arming myself with the sword of the spirit and with His righteousness. I began speaking differently too. I would pray and fast and I would ask God to lead me. Let it be His words and not my words. I knew up to this point in life, I did not always make the right decisions and honestly, I was afraid to make mistakes that may cost my child pain and suffering. Or even worse, I could lose my child. So each day I prepared myself with prayers. I would sing songs I heard on the K-LOVE radio station. They were worship songs I learned. Worship began to be my warfare. I loved music and I loved to dance. I began to sing and dance in the spirit and praise the Lord. I finally found something that made my spirit feel free. I could get lost in the music. Once I found this type of music where people were singing about how good God has been to them, I fell on my face and cried out a whole river. I found deliverance in my mind, body, and my soul. I would cry out to God in these moments. I would tell Him how angry I was. Sometimes at Him. I would be my honest self. I mean if God is all-knowing and all-seeing, He knows how I feel already. So I can be my authentic self in our conversations. This type of connection with God just grew in intensity. I could close my eyes and pray anywhere. I could calm myself during any stressful situation inside my own head. I could hear scriptures run through my mind. I began to change. I morphed into a creature of divine intervention; the Godly kind. I felt like a caterpillar who was once about to die, finally understanding that God was just preparing me for flight. I learned more about my faith and worried less about the storm. God began to show Himself in more and more situations. I learned to lean on Him when I had no understanding, when life just didn't make sense to me. You would think family court is fair and that they work for the best interest of the child, right? Wrong. They work for the best interest of their pockets. All the while your heart is in turmoil and everyone involved is being compensated for their time at the courthouse. Trust me, they are "well" compensated. They do not even consider what is best for the child. It doesn't matter. The only thing that they consider is which parent has the most money. As if that was a precursor to good parenting.

Prayer and fasting was a new thing for me. So I did some research to find out what it was about and how to properly accomplish my goals through it. Some people fast from meat, some give up their favorite things like coffee and cakes. Some people don't eat the entire time and only drink water. I looked for a verse in the Bible to teach me about fasting, trying to figure out exactly how God intended it to be. I wanted to do it exactly how God wanted it the first time around without any failures. I had no time for mistakes. I had to get it right for my children. Here's what I found:

ISAIAH 58:6:

"Isn't this the fastest that I have chosen? To lose the bands of wickedness, to undo the heavy burdens, and to let the oppressed go free, and that ye break every yoke?"

I see here that fasting is used to get rid of demons and chains, and to help the oppressed be set free! I didn't understand that initially. I needed to gain some knowledge about these things. What did they mean by chains? Is it talking about addictions, mental illness, anxiety? It must be speaking about depression too. In my case, post traumatic Stress disorder. Most people do not understand that these "chains" or "illnesses" are demonic by nature. So this tells me how important fasting is. It says, "heavy burdens." So this means it's a great sacrifice unto God. But ultimately, it removes things from me that are heavy and weighing me down. Thanks be to God.

ESTHER 4:16:

"Go, gather together all the Jews that are present in Shushan, and fast ye for me, and neither eat nor drink three days, night or day; I also and my maidens will fast likewise, and so will I go unto the King, which is not according to the law; and if I perish, I perish."

Esther teaches us to pray and fast for one another. She uses fasting so that she may have favor in the sight of God and the king in order to do something not according to the Jewish law. And she prevails! We have a lot to learn from Esther's story. She could have been killed for this. She actually risked her life to save her people. This story reminds us to be in fasting one for another and to cover each other in prayer. She taught everyone to fast with her so they were all in agreement to what she was asking of God. This is what one accord truly means. I think this is amazing, to know that other people are in agreement with you and that she found favor in God, as well as the king. I think this is an awesome lesson on fasting, faith, and trusting God.

I believe it's important to set a time to begin your day. Spend at least twenty minutes in worship and prayer. I believe your day must start out thanking God you woke up. Dedicate your work for that day to Him. You are asking Him for guidance in all you do. You could simply put on some worship music and listen during your shower. Before you know it, you are worshiping too. Then choose your fast and dedicate it unto God. No one needs to know you are fasting either. This is something personal between you and God. Stop Satan and all of his kingdom in your life, for things known and unknown. Sometimes we get ourselves mixed up with him without even knowing it! But the important thing is that you choose God above all right here and right now. Dedicate your fast to God and the casting down of all strongholds in your life and all "heavy burdens."

CHAPTER 3:

God's Grace

PROVERBS 11:16:

*"A gracious woman retaineth honor;
and a strong man retains riches."*

I began to see that I was a "Woman of God," I was worthy and honorable! I was righteous because of the lamb of God. I began to walk in the authority being led by the Holy Ghost. I walked into the courtroom like a sheep and I left it like a lamb of God, feeling like no matter what may be said about me, I walked with God's confidence that it will be "HIS WILL." Not mine, and NOT the judge's. No more fear of the unknown. No more thinking Satan will ultimately win. Even if he rules this world, it still belongs to God. And I am His daughter. I am a princess and heir to the throne of God in Heaven, created by the father. I also started to pray for the other people I met along the way. I started to understand who I was in Christ, but also why I was called to this war in the first place! Then I knew I was created for a time such as this! God began to move in a mighty way for me. Once I took my eyes off of my battles, I realized there was a whole army of soldiers that needed to put on their armor too!

PROVERBS 31:25:

"Strength and honor are her clothing,
and she shall rejoice in time to come."

Not understanding yet that God was also preparing me for work yet to come, I began to pray for everyone in the courtroom area. Moms and dads. The Judges, the clerks, the law guardians, and even the abusers. My lawyer: he needed plenty of prayer too, for all the other cases he was battling. I could see this was such a place of misery. I was also attacked in the waiting area by my abuser. He tried to assault me, throwing a punch right at my face. Thank God I learned to duck and weave and he missed me. I believe I was in the spirit too when this happened. Even really before understanding what "in the spirit" was. I did not see him coming, I didn't even see him walk up to me, and the courtroom officer did not even see it happen either because he was reading the newspaper and not even paying attention to his job. I ran up to him for help. I said, "Did you see that he just tried to punch me in the face?" The officer said very calmly, "Just sit next to me, I'll watch you." I said, "But I am not the animal, I am not the one you're supposed to watch! You need to watch him!" Of Course, I sat down. Lord knows if he would have attacked me again, it somehow would have been considered my fault, if considered at all. These courthouses are understaffed and overworked. So being in "the Spirit" at all times and being in prayer during these hearings is so important. Trusting God is what can be difficult. As survivors, we are so used to having to be the peacekeeper. We are so used to being an "action" person that to "let go and let God" can sometimes be really difficult! But I promise you that once you master this skill you will give yourself so much more room to breathe. I mean to breathe, and then to EXHALE! It is vital to your deliverance. This weight doesn't belong to you anymore. And you do not have to carry it any further. Give it to God and let Him work on it. You are not allowed to pick it back up either! This is the beginning of you gaining some faith in God. But most of all, DELIVERANCE and HEALING. There is nothing like being set free. Praise the name of Jesus.

PROVERBS 3:15:

"She is more precious than rubies, and all the things thou canst desire are not to be compared unto her."

I began to understand my position as a daughter of the Most High God. I realized how important I am to the kingdom of God and understood my value. Because of these messages in the Bible, I knew God was with me and He would not leave my side. I started to read the Bible daily. I learned to pray and ask God for a message. Then I would randomly open my Bible to a page and God would lead me right to the area He wanted me to read. It was always exactly the right message for that time in my life. I felt more and more confident that the victory was going to be mine. I learned that it first had to happen in my mind and then I had to allow God to arm me with His weapons so I could walk in faith. I mean, truly dedicating myself to God.

Chapter 4:

Prayer for Salvation

Romans 10:9-10:

"That if thou shalt confess with thy mouth the Lord Jesus. And shall believe in thine heart that God hath raised him from the dead, thou shall be saved. For with thy heart man believeth unto righteousness; and with the mouth confession is made unto salvation."

It's honestly that simple. Say that prayer and you too shall be saved. Here's another prayer:

Romans 10:13

"For whosoever shall call on the name of the Lord shall be saved."

It's that simple. So call on God. Morning, noon, and night. I believe it's through this transition that you will find your purpose. Continue to praise Him every morning. Learn to say "Thank You" at the end of the night. You should begin to speak to God day and night. Honestly, for me, He became my best friend for life. I talk to Him all day and night. Like He's right there with me. Sitting beside me. I believe He is omnipresent. He is in all places, at all times. Then when you go back to that courtroom, your defense is different. Power has shifted and you are beginning to understand faith. God is with you! Hallelujah.

CHAPTER 5:

Judgment

LUKE 12:11-12:

"And when they bring you unto the synagogues, and unto magistrates, and powers, take Ye no thought on how or what thing Ye shall answer, or what ye shall say. For the Holy Ghost shall teach you in the same hour what ye ought to say."

Believe me when I tell you this is exactly how it happens! You don't have to prepare for war, for the Holy Ghost is ready within you at all times. He will lead you to say things of certainty. And you shall prevail in all matters! But you have to be in constant prayer and fasting mode for this to take place, dedicated to reading the Word of God. It is within this renewing of your mind that your transformation takes place!

ISAIAH 54:17:

"No weapon formed against thee shall prosper, and every tongue that rises up against thee in judgment thou shall condemn. This is the heritage of the servants of the Lord, and their righteousness is of me, saith the Lord."

So right here God is telling us that no matter what the devil tries, he's not gonna win. No matter what lies he brings or what cheating he does, he still loses the battle. We have to remember that this battle belongs to God. It's spiritual in nature, therefore the only way to win it is to be ONE with GOD at all times. Allow Him to do the work for us. We have to be strengthened by the Holy Ghost, fed manna from heaven, and released from the chains around our ankles. Pray and fast constantly. I promise, you will feel God's wings around you protecting you. It's truly amazing. I joined a church. Word of God Ministries Inc. The pastor and women there began to pray and fast with me. And they still do to this day! They began to help me in this war and gave me scriptures to read. My very first one is still my favorite. Psalms 91. The pastor prayed over me and my two-year-old that day. I was told to read it at night, every night, as I was having horrible nightmares from PTSD. As the pastor began to pray, I was asked what I needed prayer for. I honestly said I didn't know. So the pastor began to pray in tongues and speak to God on my behalf. Then God told the pastor that me and my child were suffering horrible nightmares. Only God knew that. I never shared that with anyone. So it had to truly be God telling the pastor that is what we needed prayer for. Believe it or not, that night the nightmares stopped. I learned to scream out loud "JESUS," every time I felt scared. He was becoming my rock. My salvation. My world. Psalms 91. For me, it is EVERYTHING.

CHAPTER 6:

Under God's Wing

PSALMS 91:1-16

"He that dwelleth in the secret place of the most hi, shall abide under the shadow of the all mighty. I will say of the Lord, he is my refuge, my fortress; my God; in him will I trust. Surely he shall deliver thee from the snare of the fowler, and from the noisome pestilence. He shall cover thee with his feathers, and under his wings shalt thou trust; his truth shall be thy shield and buckler. Thou shall not be afraid for the terror by night; nor the arrow that flieth by day; Nor for the pestilence that walketh in darkness; nor for the destruction that wasteth at noonday A thousand shall fall at thy side, and ten thousand at thy right hand, but it shall not come nigh thee. Only with thy eyes shalt you see the reward of the wicked. Because thou hast made the Lord, which is my refuge, even the most hi thy habitation; There shall no evil befall thee. Neither shall any plague come nigh thy dwelling. For he shall give his angels charge over thee, to keep thee in all thy ways. They shall bear thee up in their hands, lest thou dash thy foot against a stone. Thou shall tread upon the lion and the adder; the young lion and the dragon shalt thou trample under feet. Because he hath set his love upon me, therefore will I deliver him; I will set him on high because he hath known my name. He shall call upon me, and I will answer him; I will be with him in times

of trouble; I will deliver him. And honor him. With long life will I satisfy him, and shew him my salvation."

PSALMS 31:1-24:

"In thee, oh Lord do I put my trust: let me never be ashamed: deliver me in thy righteousness. Bow down thine ear to me: deliver me speedily: be thou my strong rock, for a house of defense to save me. For thou art my rock and my fortress; therefore for thy name's sake lead me, and guide me. Pull me out of the net that they have laid privily for me: for thou art my strength. Into thy hands I commit my spirit; thou has redeemed me, O Lord God of truth. I have hated them that regard lying vanities: but I trust in the Lord. I will be glad and rejoice in thy mercy: for thou has considered my trouble: though has known my soul in adversaries. And has not shut me up into the hand of thy enemy: though has set my feet in a large room. Have mercy upon me, O Lord, for I am in trouble: my eyes are consumed with grief, yea, my soul and my belly. For my life is spent with grief, and my years with sighing: my strength faileth because of my iniquity, and my bones are consumed. I was reproach among all my enemies, but especially among my neighbors, and a fear to my acquaintance: they that did see me without fled from me. I am as forgotten as a dead man out of mind: I am like a broken vessel. For I have heard the slander of many: fear was on every side: while they took counsel together against me, they devised to take away my life. But I trusted in thee, O Lord: I said, Thou art my God. My times are in thy hand: deliver me from the hand of my enemies, and from them that persecute me. Make thy face

to shine upon thy servant: save me for thy mercies sake. Let me not be ashamed, O Lord: for I have called upon thee: let the wicked be ashamed, and let them be silent in the grave. Let the lying lips be put to silent: which speaketh grievous things proudly and contemptuously against the righteous. O how great is thy goodness, which though has laid up for them that fear thee: which though has wrought for them that trust in thee before the sons of man! Thou shall hide them in the secret of thy presence from the pride of man: thou shall keep them secretly in a pavilion from the strife of tongues. Blessed be the Lord: for he hath shrewd me his marvelous kindness in a strong city. For I have said in my haste I am cut off from before thy eyes: nevertheless, thou heardest the voice of my supplications when I cried unto thee. O love the Lord, all ye saints: for the Lord preserveth the faithful, and plentiful rewardeth the proud doer. Be of good courage, and he shall strengthen your heart, all ye that hope in the Lord."

PSALMS 100:1-5:

"Make a joyful noise unto the Lord, all ye lands. Serve the Lord with gladness; come before his presence with singing. Know ye that the Lord he is God. It is he that made us, and not we ourselves; we are his people and the sheep of his pasture. Enter into his gates with thanksgiving, and into his courts with praise; be thankful unto him, and bless his name. For the Lord is good, and his mercy is everlasting. And his truth endureth to all generations."

I could go on and on, but I encourage you to seek God for yourselves. Get your copy of the King James Version of the Bible. Read it! Sometimes I would be lost and cry out to God for an answer, open to a random page in the Bible, and get a word from God. I promise, He always led me to an area that helped me. Begin that relationship with God, and He will answer all your prayers! And fast for deliverance and healing. Then watch God and what He does in your situation. Get connected with a church. You need an army battling with you! Put on God's full armor.

ROMANS 10:11:

"For the scripture saith, whosoever believeth on him shall not be ashamed."

So no matter what you are going through, you are not to feel ashamed. You are a child of the highest God and He is with you. The one thing I know for sure: God don't make no junk! I know you represent heaven and God. So maybe you're not at your best right now, not in your best role in life, but you still are on the winning team. Sometimes it seems like we are losing our minds. The fear sets in and your heart starts pounding. Especially if you have to keep seeing your abuser in court hearings, or you have to take your child to some sort of visitation. It can trigger a lot inside.

So I usually go back to my happy place in my head. I take deep breaths making sure to inhale completely, allowing the total rise and fall of my chest. Then exhale completely, counting inside my head, and I would do it for a few more seconds. Usually, I'd forget why I got upset in the first place. Although sometimes I had to get up and change scenery, change my seat or even move from the whole area. I gave myself permission to do that. I kept reminding myself to remain calm and to never let them see me sweat. I had self-control. He was no longer controlling me. I had every right to be there, fighting for myself and my child, patting myself on the back, and, most of all, controlling my breathing. I refused to allow this situation to control me or the way I breathe, or to make my heart pound every time I saw my abuser. I started taking my power back day by day. I refused to let Satan make a fool out of me anymore. I used to picture him laughing at me. I wanted to laugh at him now. So I kept empowering myself. I found this organization named The Battered Women's Resource Center. I thought, Wow, there are more women out here like me. Could they be going through the same thing as me?

So I joined the organization. The group had just started. I had an interview to speak to them about my story, about how my children were kidnapped by their dad, "legally." You see, I have been to family court three separate times with three different fathers. Each case was different. I tell you; I was in court a total of seventeen years! Although each case was different, the laws were all the same. When I joined VOW, something changed inside me. I found "my tribe" of other women who were going through similar situations and having similar problems with the agencies set up to help! I learned I was not alone in this battle. And honestly, I needed them. It was my second time in family court and I was lost. I cried all the time, feeling defeated before I even showed up. But throughout my training with VOW, something changed. I grew stronger. I learned the laws and what the court looked for. I started to emulate the lawyers. I was more confident in my battle because I had warriors training me. I knew I just had to keep fighting, praying, worshiping, and fasting.

CHAPTER 7:

Prayers for Battle

Here are some prayers I found during my battles.

PROVERBS 16:7:

*"When a man's ways please the Lord, he maketh
even his enemies to be at peace with him."*

I quickly began to understand that I had to serve God
completely. No half-stepping. I could not expect God to move on
my behalf if I wouldn't move on His. God can make my enemies
to be at peace with me. That was such a powerful statement.
This God can do miracles. All I have to do is serve Him and He
will move on my behalf. Now I had to figure out what that was:
"serving." So I also joined a church and was singing in their
choir. I was praying with a women's group. Reading the words
in the Bible and then hearing it explained in church Bible study
groups made the Word of God become flesh for me. It came
alive. I began to look for God in everything I did. I saw that
He was already a part of everything I was doing. I kept reading
scriptures for battles. Even back in those days, these things

happened. So what does the Bible say about court hearings and these types of trials?

1 CORINTHIANS 6:1-10:

"Dare any of you, having a matter against another, go to law before the unjust, and not before the saints. Do ye not know that saints will judge the world? And if the world shall be judged by you, are ye unworthy to judge the smallest matters? Know ye not that we shall judge angels? How much more things pertain to this life? If then ye have judgments of things pertaining to this life, set them to judge who are least esteemed in the church. I speak to your shame. Is it so that there is not a wise man among you? No not one that shall be able to judge between his brethren? But brother goeth to law with brother, and that before the unbelievers. Now, therefore, there is utterly a fault among you, because ye go to law one with another. Why do ye rather not take wrong? Why do ye rather suffer yourselves to be defrauded? Nay, ye do wrong, and defraud, and that your brethren. Know ye not that the unrighteous shall not inherit the kingdom of God? Be ye not deceived; neither fornicators, nor idolaters, nor adulterers, nor effeminate, nor abusers of themselves with mankind. Nor thieves, nor covetous, nor drunkards, no revilers, nor extortioners, shall inherit the kingdom of God."

I began to understand that at all times, I was more afraid of misleading the judge in court than with the afterlife in heaven. I started to see that even back in the Bible people were lying and stealing and causing harm. I also began to understand that since this fight was spiritual, I had to fight like a girl, a "Daddy's Girl" that is. I also understood that even in the Bible it states the courts are filled with the lawless. So I continued to pray and fast and read the Bible daily: getting myself strengthened from the inside out and healing in my mind, my body, and my soul. Going to meetings with VOW and changing the systems women rely on was truly groundbreaking for me. It was very empowering. It was a momentous time in my life, right at the time I was fighting in court. We did training for things like public speaking. It helped to know I was NOT alone in this injustice in family court. I began to see the overwhelming amount of women fighting my very same fight. Having to prove to the court that we are "good" mothers. Whether it was in criminal courtrooms, Administration for Children's Services courtrooms, family court, child support court, or divorce court. I mean, sheesh, there is a courtroom for everything. Now we have an IDV court, Integrated Domestic Violence court, to hear cases that may have gone from custody and visitation to now being in criminal court also. There was a shift in courthouses. We can now combine those cases and hear the criminal case before the judge even considers visitations or custody matters. It is a one-stop shop for Domestic Violence survivors. Though, it sometimes feels like they want to hurry up the criminal case so they can move on to visitations. You can also get tricked here. Like I was told to drop the criminal case and he would drop the visitation case. Little did I know he would pick it back up a year later.

1 TIMOTHY 8:8-11:

"But we know that the law is good if a man uses it lawfully; Knowing this, that the law is not made for a righteous man, but for the lawless and disobedient, for the ungodly and for sinners, for unholy, and profane, for murders of fathers and murders of mothers, for manslayers, For whoremongers, for them that defile themselves with mankind, for menstealers, for liars, for perjured persons, and if there be any other things that is contrary to sound doctrine: According to the glorious gospel of the blessed God, which was committed to my trust."

God's word teaches us to expect the unexpected. Court victory starts with prayers.

EZEKIEL 46:21:

"Then he brought me forth into the utter court, and caused me to pass by the four corners of the court; and behold, in every corner of the court, there was a court."

This to me says that we will face many judgments here in this world. So as for me and my house, we will serve the Lord.

Stay connected to the source.

JOSHUA 24:14-15:

"Now, therefore, fear the Lord, and serve him in sincerity and in truth; and put away the Gods which your fathers served on the other side of the flood, and in Egypt; and serve ye the Lord. And if it seems evil unto you to serve the Lord, choose you this day whom ye will serve; whether the Gods which your fathers served that were on the other side of the flood or the Gods of the Amorites, in whose land ye dwell; but as for me and my house, we will serve the Lord."

You have to sincerely make a choice. Because even if you do not choose, you have still made a choice. God tells us it is better to be an enemy than to be lukewarm. You have to pick a side, simple as that. Renounce Satan, and all of his kingdom, and run into your Daddy's arms! Our father God will never let you down. It's in this transition that you learn to trust God; run fast, quick, and jump! This is the beginning of God removing the veil from your eyes. Do not be surprised when you wake up one day and everything seems different. Honestly, it is. Because YOU are different. You are finding your inner strength. You are learning how to battle. You are fully covered in the armor of God and you are walking in God's strength. He renews it daily.

EPHESIANS 4:31:

*"Let all bitterness, and wrath and anger, and clamor, and
evil speaking, be put away from you, with all malice."*

At this point, I began to understand I needed to give my heart
completely to God. Because I was still very angry and hurting.
I needed to learn how to find forgiveness for someone or some
situations that did not deserve it. But in finding forgiveness, I
forgave myself. I stopped blaming myself. I asked God to help
me find peace in the storm. I started to understand why I stayed
so long. Why did I continue to try to fix this broken person?
Even when it hurt me. I stayed. I blamed myself for a lot more
than I realized. Even after I separated, I could still hear my ex's
nasty comments replaying in my head. So once and for all, I had
to stop them. I continued to pray and fast. I found time every
morning to dedicate time to God. I started a daily routine and
found that adding God was truly life-altering. Then at the end
of the day, I would say, "Thank you, Father, for allowing me
another day above ground." I would try to find things to be
grateful for. Like that fact I had a roof over my head, I ate that
day, and I was still somewhat in my right state of mind. I would
thank God for spending my day with me. I began to feel Him
always there. I also began going to therapy. That was crucial
for my healing. Trauma informed therapy helped me understand

myself and my choices. Then at my VOW meetings, I was more and more empowered. I found a healthy balance in life: eating healthy, exercising, and praying. Prayers, prayers, prayers, never ending prayers.

CHAPTER 8:

Renounce Satan and His Kingdom

EPHESIANS 5:11:

*"And have no fellowship with the unfruitful
works of darkness, but rather reprove them."*

This is why I say you must renounce Satan and all his works! Don't keep doing the foolish things of the past. You must start using wisdom in all areas of your life. Sometimes we get used to being with certain demons. Like we may have a fascination with earning money, not realizing that worshiping money is unhealthy. God should be your provider and if you worship Him, He provides for all your needs. Or some of us overeat. You might not think much of this. *Oh well, I eat a lot when I am nervous!* But actually, it's a form of gluttony. Or maybe we have an addiction to shopping? Maybe it makes us feel good, without us realizing its vanity. There are so many little things we may have been doing for years without understanding how it may be harming us. We have to ask God to take a full inventory of our

32

hearts to help us get rid of things seen and unseen.

Ephesians 5:14:

"Wherefore he saith, Awake thou that sleepest, and arise from the dead, and Christ shall give thee light."

These are very powerful prayers! God is going to awaken in you that which He has placed inside. You're going to become a new creature in Christ. All God asks of you is that you try. Reach out to Him for support and guidance and He will strengthen you. Read the Bible daily and fast. It's honestly that simple.

Romans 8:28:

"And we know that all things work together for the good to them that love God, to them who are called according to his purpose."

Right here God is letting us know that everything we are going through is somehow created for our good: maybe growth in the spirit or growth in your faith. One day you will look back and see why it was necessary. I promise, then it will all make so much sense. You will see how God took these horrible storms and used them for His glory and His purpose in your life. I know that when you're drowning and you can't see the land you panic. But learning to trust God and lean on His promises is all you really need to do right now. Then He will have you walk on water. Hallelujah!

Chapter 9:

Closing Remarks

Corinthians 13:13:

*"And now abideth in faith, hope, charity, these three:
but the greatest of these is charity [love]."*

Thank you, Father God, that you love your people so much that even unto this day you abide in us. You make the way straight. You are in control. I love that this verse is letting us know what is expected of us as we seek God and His kingdom. Love yourselves and each other. You are now spiritually awakened. There's no going back! The blinders have been removed but it's up to you what you do with this information. I pray that you find yourself in a church. Preferably a Christian Church that uses the King James Version of the Bible. A church that believes in the fruits of the spirit. A fivefold ministry. One thing I know for sure: this battle IS of a spiritual nature, and now that you have gone through the steps in this prayer guide on how to be "set free" I am believing God has already begun to move in your lives, that the veil is torn, and you can now see in the spiritual realm. But I warn you, stay in prayer and fasting for yourselves.

As you begin this journey, always remember to seek God for yourself. You have to have a personal relationship with Him. You have to pray to Him daily. It is as simple as communication. No fancy words are needed. Just an open heart to give and also allow God to give back to you and communicate. Set aside time throughout your day. I speak with my "Daddy" all throughout the day. Morning, noon, and night. I don't want to do anything that is not in His will for me. And He responds to me. Sometimes it may be through a song or perhaps a person. God will always respond to you. You have to be awake to hear from Him though. Find ways to serve God. Like volunteering with the homeless, veterans hospitals, or maybe the Humane Society. Go play with a doggie! There is no job too big, nor too small when serving God. Each one of us has a calling. You have to figure out what yours is. And then go for it. I plead the blood of Jesus over your lives, I plead the blood over your situations. God's got it ALL!

About the Author

Dana Hanuszczak is a dedicated advocate and survivor of domestic violence and childhood trauma. After experiencing the revictimization that often occurs within the systems survivors turn to for help, Dana has devoted her life to improving those very systems. As a lead organizer with Voices of Women (VOW), she spearheads initiatives such as the Police Reform Project and the Emergency Housing Voucher Project. She also serves as the intake and outreach service coordinator at VOW.

Dana's advocacy extends beyond VOW. She has worked with the NYC Mayor's Office to End Gender-Based Violence as part of the "Voices Committee," where she amplified the voices of domestic violence survivors. She is also involved with Faith In New York, an organization led by the NYC Mayor's office, and has worked as an Emergency Medical Technician (EMT) in New York for over fifteen years. Dana is certified in mental health crisis counseling and drug and alcohol addiction, providing essential services to those in need.

As a primary counselor in an alternatives to incarceration program, Dana has assisted parents in reunifying with their children after intervention by the Administration for Children's Services. She is a fierce advocate for systemic change, leading survivors to legislative action in Albany to push for laws that protect survivors of domestic violence. She recognizes that many survivors end up incarcerated for actions taken in self-defense and works to address these injustices.

Dana is also a Chaplain, volunteering at the Women's Reception Center Prison Ministry. Her work with criminalized survivors extends to her role as a consultant with CUNY ISLG. Her personal experiences as a former gang member and troubled youth give her a unique perspective in mentoring at-risk youth and creating safe spaces for difficult conversations.

In addition to her advocacy and counseling work, Dana facilitates a survivor support group and engages in discussions around diversity, inclusion, and language barriers. Fluent in Spanish, she bridges gaps in communities of color, where disparities in support services are often exacerbated by language barriers.

Dana's commitment to healing is holistic, focusing on the mind, body, and spirit. Since relocating to Florida, she has founded the nonprofit Survivor Center to address the lack of services for domestic violence survivors in Volusia County, which has some of the highest rates of domestic violence and homicides in the state. Her journey continues her forthcoming autobiography, *Becoming Savage Angel*.

Printed in the USA
CPSIA information can be obtained
at www.ICGtesting.com
LVHW021505081124
796013LV00009B/182

* 9 7 9 8 8 9 3 3 3 9 3 9 0 *